MW00414948

The Making Of A King

The Making Of A King

Transforming Boys into Men

JEFFREY A. JOHNSON, SR.

TATE PUBLISHING
AND ENTERPRISES, LLC

Published by Tate Publishing & Enterprises, LLC
127 E. Trade Center Terrace | Mustang, Oklahoma 73064 USA
1.888.361.9473 | www.tatepublishing.com

Tate Publishing is committed to excellence in the publishing industry. The company reflects the philosophy established by the founders, based on Psalm 68:11,
"The Lord gave the word and great was the company of those who published it."

Book design copyright © 2015 by Tate Publishing, LLC. All rights reserved.
Cover design by Maria Louella Mancao
Interior design by Jake Muelle

Published in the United States of America

ISBN: 978-1-68187-567-5
1. Religion / Christian Life / Inspirational
2. Religion / Christian Life / Family
15.08.07

Dedicated to all of the young
men who don't yet know
that they were born to be kings.
May God inspire you
to find His purpose for your lives.

Contents

Foreword

It's not easy raising children. It never has been. And it probably never will be. As a father of six, I know this from firsthand experience. The raising of boys is particularly challenging because we aren't just raising boys, we're shaping the lives of kings. In writing *The Making of a King: Transforming Boys into Men,* Pastor Jeffrey Johnson relies upon both personal life experiences and the knowledge that comes from raising four boys. In this, his seventh published work, he uses personal stories, pertinent illustrations, and the power of God's Word to remind us that boys can be kings no matter what obstacles life may bring.

The Making of a King begins with a discussion about the King of Kings and the fact that accepting Christ makes us a part of the royal priesthood. According to Pastor Johnson:

> The enemy cannot tell who is going to be king or not be king because all of you have kingly potential. All of you have kingly possibilities. The Bible says that when we put our faith in Jesus, we become part of a royal priesthood. But how does that translate into our personal lives?

Using the life of King Josiah, found in 2 Kings 22, Pastor Johnson shows how this priesthood can be lived out. He walks us through the challenges and issues of everyday life, ranging from delinquency to brokenness to fatherlessness. He reminds us that everybody has dysfunction in his or her life. He discusses the importance of mentorship and looking up to others as well as having the right attitude and the right focus. He states that becoming a king requires getting into the Word of God and being active in a local church.

I have the privilege not only of calling Pastor Jeffrey Johnson a colleague in ministry, but he is also a very dear friend. As such, God has allowed me to witness his life up close and on a personal level. He lives what he shares, and he shares what he lives. What he has written in his *Dialogue* series and now in *The Making of a King* reflects his heart for people and the Kingdom of God.

I encourage you to read this book. Tell your relatives, friends, and acquaintances to read it. And begin the work of helping the boys in your life be transformed into kings.

—Pastor John K. Jenkins, Sr.
Senior Pastor, First Baptist
Church of Glenarden

Preface

Josiah was eight years old when he became king, and he reigned in Jerusalem thirty-one years. His mother's name was Jedidah daughter of Adaiah; she was from Bozkath. He did what was right in the eyes of the LORD and followed completely the ways of his father David, not turning aside to the right or to the left.

(2 Kings 22:1-2)

When I read these verses from 2 Kings, I was struck by the fact that this portion of Scripture was talking about a boy who took on a man's responsibility when he was just eight years old. And what's more, "he did what was right in the eyes of the Lord."

As a father of four sons, I wondered what happened in this boy's life that enabled him to take on such an enormous responsibility and do it in a way that pleased the watchful eyes of the Lord. What was the role of his father in the making of this king? What was the role of his mother? Who influenced him? How did this happen?

I studied this passage to find out not only what specific things worked in Josiah's life to turn a young boy into a king, but also to find out what *principles* might have been at work. What can we learn from the story of Josiah that would enable us today to turn our young boys into kings? This little book presents what I learned about *the making of a king*.

Genesis 1:26 (KJV) reads, "And God said, Let us make man in our image, after our likeness: and let them have dominion...." In God's original design of man, he intended for man to have dominion. (Let me be clear that "man" in this verse actually stands for humankind, not just males. Verse 27 goes on to say, "...male and female created he them." So God intends for both men and women to have dominion. But since this book is about helping to transform boys into men, please allow me to focus here on what this means for men.)

God's desire is for man to rule and reign like a king. From the beginning, God has ordained man with the authority to be victorious in a diversity of areas. It is clear, however, that men are not born but made: "Let us make man." There is the divine possibility to be transformed from boyhood to manhood. Any boy can be made into a man with the anointing to rule over the areas of life that God has designed for him to have dominion. You can help yourself or any boy you know to reign over the spiritual, physical, psychological, emotional, intellectual, sexual, financial, and other areas of life. It's never too early or too late to begin. Let us take boys and make them into men so that they may rule like kings.

Kings Are a Threat

Jesus Christ was the only One who was ever born King. Every other king had to be made—but not Jesus. He was King before He got here, He was King while He was here, and He will be King forevermore. When Jesus was born, a man named Herod who was king of the Jews felt threatened by everybody. He was so insecure that whenever he thought people wanted to usurp his authority and take his crown, he simply got rid of them—including his family members. So when he heard that a baby was born "King of the Jews," he sought to kill this baby named Jesus.

The only problem was that he didn't know where to find the baby, so he called for the religious leaders—the priests and scribes. He asked them, "What do the Scriptures say about where this newborn king will be found?" They told him that He would be found in Bethlehem, so that's where Herod sent his men to take out this newborn king. The challenge of those orders was that Herod and his men couldn't tell which boy in Bethlehem was that king. That's why Herod commanded that all of the little boys in Bethlehem who were two years of age and under be killed immediately. He couldn't just look at a boy and tell whether or not he would be king because all of the boys had kingly potential.

Likewise, the Enemy cannot tell who will be king or not because all of us have kingly potential. The Bible says that when we put our faith in Jesus, we become part of a royal priesthood. But how does that translate into our personal lives? How can we flesh that out? How can we express this kingly potential? How can we live that out so that we can be the kings that God is calling us to be?

Delinquents
in the Making

A few years ago, Harvard University conducted a research study from which they discovered that it's possible to predict which children will become juvenile delinquents, based on certain determining factors. One major way to tell if a child is on his way to becoming a delinquent involves paternal absence. Whether or not the father has custody of the child, he must at least be involved in his child's life. When the father is not there at all, the child is well on his way to becoming a delinquent.

Another factor they discovered is that when there's no discipline in the home, a child may well become a delinquent. When

21

we parents do not set boundaries and are not firm, fair, and consistent in our discipline, our children may be on their way to becoming delinquents.

The researchers said another sign is that the parents do not know their children's friends. In other words, we can't just send our children out the door. Instead, we have to ask them, "Who are your friends?" We have to say, "Bring your friends in so that we can meet them."

The study also said that children may be on their way to delinquency when the parents don't know where they are. There should not be a minute that passes by when we don't know where our children are. We need to tell them, "I need to know where you're going to be and who you're going to be with." When I was a kid, there was a popular radio station that asked every night at ten o'clock, "Do you know where your children are?" We parents need to constantly ask that of ourselves and be sure we know the answer.

Especially in the twenty-first century, when we are doing FaceTime with everyone else, we need to also be doing some FaceTime with our children. In terms of today's technology, we need to know every password our children have. We need to go to Facebook and make a friend request to our children. Then, with their password, we have to go to that page, accept ourselves as a friend, and regularly log on to see with whom our children are connecting. Unless we stay on top of that crucial information, we may find our children straying into harmful relationships and unhealthy places. We must realize that our children are not automatically exempt from becoming delinquents just because we are Christian parents.

As residents of the United States, we know how the penal system here works. The penal institutions—the jails and prisons—determine how many beds to obtain for their facilities based on the reading levels of third-graders. In essence, when a third-grader cannot read, another bed is added to a prison, awaiting that child's arrival at some point in the future.

Disciples Instead
of Delinquents

As I read about this Harvard study, I thought, *Now, if we can* predict *delinquency, we should be able to* prevent *delinquency*. If we know what it takes for a child to become a delinquent, we ought to replace those criteria with standards that will make that child into a disciple of Christ instead. If we know, for instance, that being illiterate is going to land a person in jail, instead of adding a bed to a facility, why don't we just teach that child to read?

If we take care of our children on the front end, we won't have to worry about them on the back end. If we provide them with an education on the front end, we won't have to provide incarceration on the back end. Maybe the problem is that we invest only fourteen thousand dollars into their education on the front end, but then we invest fifty thousand dollars into their incarceration on the back end. It's time for us to stand up and help our boys to become men, disciples not delinquents—kings. We need to help them become the persons God intends for them to be.

It can indeed happen. Josiah demonstrates that concept to us in 2 Kings 22. Not only did he become king when he was eight and rule for thirty-one years, but he also became one of the greatest kings in Israel's history. Because of Josiah's restoration of the house of God and reformation of the nation of Israel, he ranks among Israel's greatest leaders, right up there with David and Solomon.

Dysfunction
Is No Excuse

The intriguing fact about Josiah rising to such greatness is that he came from a dysfunctional family. Some of us use our family background as an excuse—right? We say such things as, "I can't live out my royalty… I can't live out my prosperity…I can't be successful…I can't live out my destiny… because I'm from a dysfunctional family. Because my father walked out on us, my mother had to work two jobs just to put food on our table. So it's no wonder that I can't be what I'm supposed to be. I'm from a dysfunctional family."

But wait a minute! *Everybody* is from a dysfunctional family. There's no such thing as a perfect family. Now, I agree that there are different *levels* of dysfunction, but we all come from dysfunctional families. None of us can put up a sign in our yard that says, "No Dysfunction Here." Everybody has something going on in the home that ought not to be going on. Therefore, we can't use our dysfunctional family background as an excuse for not becoming the men God wants us to be.

Josiah is showing us that we *can* become kings. His father, Amon, and his grandfather, Manasseh, both did evil in the sight of God. But then, the Bible tells us that Josiah did what was *right* in the sight of God. Even when his father and grandfather were wrong, he was still right. Likewise, we don't have to be wrong because our people were wrong.

Josiah's father and grandfather were so messed up that they both became idolaters. (Idolatry isn't just about worshiping a golden calf. Anything that we worship instead of God is an idol.) Amon and Manasseh worshiped *things* instead of God. Not only that, but Josiah's father was also a murderer. He killed one person after another until finally his own officials killed him in his home. Can you imagine that? He was the king of Israel, but his own people who were supposed to be supporting him killed him at home. Even though he was ruling in the kingdom, he was killed at home.

In the same way, out in the community we're movers and shakers, but at home we feel like nothing because our own families are dysfunctional. Nevertheless, we need to learn this valuable lesson from Josiah, who, even in the midst of that dysfunctional atmosphere, did what was right in the sight of God. He was able to do good even though his father was doing evil, enacting positive change even though his father was carrying out negative deeds.

One of the great things about Christianity is that we don't have to be like those who came before us. Romans 10:13 tells us, "Everyone who calls on the name of the Lord will be saved." Thus, even though our fathers may be wrong, we can still be right.

Re-"gene"-eration
Is Possible

One of the words that the Bible uses to describe salvation is "regeneration." The base word there is "gene." We know that our fathers pass on certain genes to us. That's why we not only can have similar physical characteristics, but we can also have a predisposition for certain behavior. We may say, "My father was an alcoholic," "My father was a gambler," "My father was unfaithful to his wife," "My father didn't take care of his children," or "My father wasn't in my life or the lives of my sister and brothers." We can have a predisposition towards those negative behaviors since we inherited our fathers' genes. For instance, research studies have consistently shown that the children of alcoholics are seven times more likely to become alcoholics than those whose parents were not alcoholics.

But I'm not filled with alcohol; instead, I'm filled with the Spirit. I have been re-"gene"-erated. Yes, I've got my father's bad genes, but when I placed my faith in Jesus Christ, I received the seed of God within me. As the apostle said in 1 John 3:9, "No one who is born of God will continue to sin, because God's seed remains in them; they cannot go on sinning, because they have been born of God." Because that seed of God has re-gene-d me, I don't have to be like my earthly father, but I can rather be like my heavenly Father. Even if our fathers did what was wrong, we can still do what was right.

Adult Responsibility Can Come at Any Age

Josiah became king even when his responsibility was greater than his maturity. He was just eight years old when his father died. The officials took the crown off the dead king's head and put it on the head of an eight-year-old boy. As a little boy, Josiah had a crown that was bigger than his head. In other words, his responsibility was bigger than his maturity. He was a boy with a man's responsibility.

You may now find yourself in a situation in which *your* responsibility is greater than your maturity. Even as a young boy, you may have had to do things that the *man* of the house should have been doing. You may be a father even now while you are still a child. You may only be fifteen years old and the father of two children. That's an adult responsibility, but at fifteen, you still are not quite a man. Some teenagers have to go to work, not to get a little spending money to go out with friends, but to bring home a paycheck to help support the family because of the situation in the home. Those are boys with adult responsibilities.

You may be an adult male, and in the midst of the economic downturn, your company downsized. Even though you were able to keep your job, they added the responsibilities of other positions that were eliminated. So you are now carrying responsibility for which you have not been trained and are not experienced. You have the responsibility but not the mentality to handle it.

You may have gotten married thinking marriage was one thing, but now you've discovered it's something else. Pastor Freddie Haynes says, "You thought marriage was an *ideal* but found out it was an *ordeal*, so now you're thinking you got a *raw* deal and you're out trying to find a *new* deal." When you look at your wife and what is being asked of you as a husband, you may feel that your responsibility is greater than your maturity.

When the Crown Doesn't Fit Your Head

So, here's the question: How do you handle that? How do you deal with it when the crown doesn't fit your head? How do you handle it on the job, in the home, or in your relationships when your immaturity is keeping you from handling your responsibility? It may be a mental or physical immaturity, but it could also be spiritual. Our responsibility is great, but our maturity—in one area or another—is so small.

Here's what Josiah did: he grew up! Sadly, we too often simply *give* up. When our responsibility is greater than our maturity, we shouldn't give up; instead, we should just grow up. We must grow into the crown

until the crown fits our head. As the poet
Edgar Guest wrote,

> When things go wrong, as they
>   sometimes will
> When the road you're trudging
>   seems all uphill
> When the funds are low and the
>   debts are high
> And you want to smile, but you
>   have to sigh
> When care is pressing you down
>   a bit
> Rest if you must, but don't you
>   quit....
>
> Success is failure turned inside out
> The silver tint of the clouds of
>   doubt
> And you never can tell how close
>   you are
> It may be near when it seems afar;

So stick to the fight when you're
hardest hit
It's when things seem worst that
you mustn't quit.

We can't quit because we don't know
how close we are to receiving the thing that
God has for us. So, rather than give up, we
have to grow up.

"Give Us Time"

I've been the pastor of Eastern Star Church in Indianapolis, Indiana, for twenty-six years. When I was called there, I was twenty-five years old. At the time, I wasn't really what the church was looking for. They had gone through a difficult period during which they had dismissed three different preachers in five years. They had been taken to court by one pastor, and they even had to change the locks on the church because of another pastor. Subsequently, they had tumult in the church, even resulting in fistfights. That was the kind of church God was calling me to pastor.

Yet the people on the search committee really didn't want to call me to pastor there. They told me it wasn't my level of education, because I had a good education. They told me it wasn't a lack of experience, because I had previously pastored another church. They said honestly, "You're just too young. You're only twenty-five years old. Look at the storm we've been going through. We're in a mess. We just don't think that you have the level of maturity to deal with this responsibility." I responded to them, "If your issue is my age, then all I've got to do is stay alive. If I don't jump off a bridge, put a bullet through my head, or slit my wrist, then chances are good that the maturity is going to come."

Isaiah 40:31 (KJV) tells us, "But they that wait upon the Lord shall renew their strength; they shall mount up with wings as eagles; they shall run, and not be weary; and they shall walk, and not faint." We don't give up; instead, we just grow up. And I'm a witness that God will blow it up—He will do more than we could even imagine. At the same time, we must realize that moving on into our destiny isn't going to be easy.

Not Our Fault

Josiah became king despite the difficulties he had to confront. An eight-year-old child whose father was gone, he found himself facing adult responsibilities—and his crown didn't fit his head. Yet this wasn't a result of anything that he had done. Becoming a king wasn't his decision. Instead, he was merely living with the consequences of somebody else's bad choices.

This can so easily become our predicament too. It wasn't our fault that our parents' marriage fell apart. We didn't make our father walk out. We weren't sitting in the board room or in the CEO's chair when bad decisions led to the company downsizing and the subsequent loss of our job.

We're just living with the consequences of someone else's bad choices.

Josiah found himself in the midst of a crisis. He was eight years old but had no masculine role model in the home to teach him how to be a man. When you're a child and there is no one in the home for you to model your life after, no one to help you become the man you're supposed to be, that's a crisis.

I celebrate every father who is involved in his children's lives. I am so thankful that even when some men have been divorced from their wives, they didn't divorce their children. I celebrate the men who, even though they don't have custody of the children, still provide for them—financially, spiritually, physically, emotionally, educationally, and in all ways that they need a father. I celebrate these men!

The United States, however, is in the throes of a dire crisis because of the absenteeism of fathers from the home. Too many men are AWOL from their families. Eighty percent of the African-American babies are born to single parents. And all too often, the father doesn't stick around to help raise his own children. In fact, the average amount of time a man in the United States spends with his children is seven minutes a day.

Indeed, we're in the midst of a crisis. That's why we see the outward results of this situation within our communities. All of the violence, drug addiction, drug-dealing, crime, prison recidivism, alcoholism, and rape are manifestations of what happens when a father is not in the child's life. The Harvard University research study is right. When there is paternal absence, delinquency is on the way.

A Crown in the Midst of Crisis

Some man may say, "But that's what I've been trying to tell people. That's why I am the way I am. I didn't have a male role model in the home. That's why I'm doing all of these things." No, it doesn't have to be that way. Josiah was still able to become king in spite of that paternal absence from his life. In fact, it was in the midst of his crisis that he got his crown. He didn't get the crown until after the crisis showed up.

Some of us don't understand that when we go through a crisis, it doesn't mean that God has forsaken us. It may rather mean that God is getting ready to crown us king. Sometimes God lets us go through calamities to build our character, and struggles to develop our strength. It was only when Josiah's father was removed that Josiah began to reign. God may well be getting ready to raise us up to a place we would never have reached unless we had gone through the hell at that point in our lives. God uses the difficulty to develop us and take us to our destiny.

Where Does the Rage Come From?

In Indianapolis, we have an annual conference for African-American men. The organizers bring in successful black men from a wide variety of professions—doctors, educators, pastors, administrators, businessmen, attorneys, judges— who can serve as vital role models for younger black men to emulate. At this conference, we have group conversations with young men in their teens and early twenties. Some of those boys are great students, while others have terrible grades. Some are on the verge of graduating from high school, and others have already dropped out. Some are trying to get their lives together, but others are drug dealers and gangbangers. The vision of this conference is that if these boys can hear the stories of successful black men, it will inspire them to grow into the men they can be.

At the last conference, the conversation started, and we could really feel the tension in the room. Bitter anger was emanating from the young people, and it got really hot in there. One of the members of my church who was with me leaned over and asked, "Pastor, where does such rage come from in people who are so young?" I didn't answer him then because I was focused on the conversation in case I was called upon to offer a response. But I do have an answer to this question: Where is all this bitterness and rage coming from?

Inner Brokenness

In Mooresville, Indiana, a woman discovered that her baby had a fever. The mother tried various things, but she couldn't break the fever of her three-month-old baby. So, she grabbed her baby and rushed the child to Riley Children's Hospital, one of the best children's hospitals in America, just a few miles away from her home.

The doctors began to run tests to find the cause of the fever. When they took x-rays, they found out that six different bones in that baby had been broken. The heat coming from the outside of the baby was a sign that there was brokenness on the inside. Of course, the authorities were called in, and while investigating, they found out that on three different occasions, the father had broken bones in his baby's body. That's why the baby was so hot.

So, where is all the hot bitterness and rage coming from? It's because so many men's lives have been broken by their fathers. Something their fathers did or did not do left them broken. The greater tragedy is that so many men base their manhood on their "hotness." They think that they are men because they are hot in their conversations, hot in how they relate to others, hot in the way they deal with their women, hot in the way they carry themselves, and hot in every aspect of their lives.

But being hot isn't a sign of manhood; instead, it's a sign of brokenness. These men are using their brokenness to define their manhood. Yet our manhood is not based on our brokenness—how hot we are—but on the fact that Jesus has healed our brokenness. We believe that since Jesus died on the cross for us and God raised Him from the dead, He is able to heal our brokenness. Our Savior is able to heal our fever and put our lives back together again.

Not Everyone
Walked Out

In 2 Kings 22, we learn the name of Josiah's mother, whom we don't meet until after his father is gone. We read about the father and grandfather, but we don't read anything about the mother until the father is out of the picture. Then we learn that his mother's name is Jedidah. Now Josiah is identified with his mother, not his father.

In Josiah's time, for a boy to be identified with his mother was unheard of. The Hebrew boys were readily identified through their fathers. You remember reading about "the son of Abraham," "the son of David," "the sons of Zebedee"—identification with the father. But Josiah's father was no longer there, so now he's being identified by his mother. Jedidah's name means "darling." So, Josiah is not identified by the deranged disposition of his daddy, but the darling disposition of his mother.

In preparation for my latest book, *Dialogue with Single Parents*, I invited a group of single women to come together for a conversation because I wanted to make sure I was accurately addressing their issues. Before we dismissed that meeting, the women asked me to say something. They pointed out that they had been very transparent about sharing their experiences and their feelings, and much of what they shared was very sad and difficult. But now they wanted me to say something that they could carry with them as they went back home, into that situation.

No Longer
Under the Influence

What I told them was that when my dad walked out and left my mother with four children to raise alone, it was both the worst and best thing that could have happened to me. It was the worst because boys need their fathers in the home to model what real manhood is all about.

On the other hand, it was the best thing that could have happened because I was no longer exposed to my father's attitude, disposition, and behavior. I didn't then internalize his negative influences in my own life. Had he stayed any longer than he did, I would not be preaching the gospel today. I would be out drinking, acting the fool, being unfaithful to my wife, and living my life without Jesus. But when my earthly father stepped out of my life, my heavenly Father stepped in. Of course, He had been there all the time, but I didn't realize my need for Him until then.

Josiah would not be identified by the deranged attitude of his father, but by the darling attitude of his mother. No wonder he went on to become a great man and king.

We need to learn to thank God for the women He brings into our lives. Whether it's our mother, grandmother, wife, girl-friend, sister, aunt—whoever she is—when God blesses us with a good woman, we need to appreciate that. Some of us would not be *where* we are or *who* we are had it not been for the women who provided a positive, godly influence in our lives.

Becoming an MVP

When Josiah's father left, his mother was forced to change roles because her responsibilities had changed. She not only had to take on the traditional role of the mother, but that of the father as well since he wasn't coming back. Even today, whether the man is dead or simply a deadbeat, he isn't coming back. So the mother has to change roles, expanding her responsibilities in order to try to make up at least some of the lack in her child's life.

Sometimes our relationships don't turn out the way we want them to. When we get married, most of us don't ever think about that marriage ending in divorce. We vow to stay married "till death do us part." But things happen, and some marriages end in divorce. Nevertheless, that isn't the time to throw in the towel. Your role may have to change and your responsibilities may expand, but you must not let change cause you to quit.

Magic Johnson came into the NBA in 1979. As a rookie, he went to the Lakers, and became part of what used to be called "the Lakers family." He was a 6-foot-9 point guard, the first of his kind. Today we have a lot of big guards who can handle the ball, but Magic was the very first one. Kareem Abdul-Jabbar, also on that team, was the center of what was happening in the Lakers family. They made it all the way to the finals during Magic's rookie year, and that is when Kareem Abdul-Jabbar got injured.

With the center of the family down, the coach went to Magic and essentially said, "I'm going to need you to change roles. I know that all this time you've been playing point guard, but I need you to play center tonight. We're not going to get the victory unless you change roles."

Thankfully, Magic didn't say, "I don't care what happened. I signed up to be the point guard. I'm not going through any role changes. I'm not going to step into that center role and make a fool of myself." He knew that if he was going to get the victory, he had to change roles. In his first night as center, he scored forty-two points, pulled down twelve rebounds, dished out seven assists, and brought the ultimate victory. The team won the championship because Magic stepped up when a key member of the family went down.

All kinds of unpredictable circum-stances can happen in our families, so when something goes down, we have to step up. Magic went on to become the MVP.

We need men today who will step up and become an MVP—not Most Valuable Player, but Most Valuable *Parent*. We need to do whatever it takes in the lives of our sons so that they can become kings.

Attitude or Gratitude?

Josiah was eight years old when he became king. Ironically, I was also eight years old when my father walked out on our family. When Josiah's father was removed, he started reigning and ruling. When *my* father was removed, however, I went to ruin. I got angry but didn't realize the extent of my anger. My behavior and grades at school changed for the worse. At the time, I didn't know what was going on within me. I didn't realize the brokenness within me was making me hot. I should have been like Josiah—not ruined but ruling—but I was focusing on the absence of my father instead of the presence of my mother.

If we aren't careful, we can spend so much time focusing on what we don't have in our lives anymore that we forget what we still have. I was seeing paternal absence when I should have been seeing maternal presence. I was seeing the bad habits of my father when I should have been seeing the good heart of my mother. I was seeing the sin of my father when I should have been seeing the salvation of my mother. I was seeing the perversion of my father when I should have been seeing the perseverance of my mother. I was heading to ruin because I was asking the wrong question.

It's okay to question God. We're not going to ask God anything that He can't answer. We aren't going to ask God something that's going to trip Him up and throw Him off His game. Even Jesus questioned His Father. When He was dying on the cross for your sins and mine, He cried out, "My God, My God, why have you forsaken Me?" So my problem wasn't that I was questioning God; it's just that I was asking the *wrong* question. I was asking, "God, why did my father leave?" What I should have been asking was, "How did my mother stay?"

If I could have focused on my mother's staying power, I wouldn't have been tripping over the fact that my father left. I should have been asking, "How did Mama raise four children by herself? How did Mama get all four of us through high school by herself? How did Mama pay my tuition for me to go to college? How did Mama, *with four children*, work two jobs and go back to school to get a nursing degree to become an RN in order to better provide for her children? How did Mama keep us in church? How did Mama help all of us to know Jesus as our personal Savior? How did Mama stay, persevere, put a roof over our heads, clothe us, and feed us? How

did she do it?" If we're going through difficult times, we need to learn how to ask the
right questions.

Give Credit
Where It's Due

We may look up to successful Christian men we know, such as pastors, teachers, or coaches. We see them in their suits and ties, able to talk in front of people, having gained some sort of reputation for "success" in whatever field they are in, and we're thinking, *Wow! They've got it together*. But we need to be careful that we're not giving *men* the credit that should be going to the Holy Spirit. What we're seeing is not these men operating in their own power. Instead, we're witnessing what happens when men place their faith in Jesus and the Holy Spirit moves in and empowers them to accomplish the things that He wants to do through them. Indeed, sometimes we give too much credit to a person and not enough to the Holy Spirit.

Paul George is our starting shooting guard on the Indiana Pacers, and he's the real deal. He can play really well. He was playing for the USA team, representing us in international basketball, when he suffered a nasty break and had to be carted off the floor. He was told then that his break was so bad that he wouldn't be able to play in the 2014-15 season. But when we got to the first home game and were looking at the players warming up on the court shooting baskets, Paul George was out there with them. Now, he didn't play that night, but the very thought that he could even be out there on the court walking around after that horrible incident was amazing. He had his uniform on and was taking shots at the basket while messing around with his teammates, and the crowd loved it.

The media went wild. They were talking on Twitter, blogging, and getting the word out that Paul George was in the house. A sportscaster who interviewed Larry Bird, president of basketball operations for the Indiana Pacers, remarked, "We saw Paul George out there on the court shooting jumpers. He looked good." Bird responded, "Don't put too much into that. His leg is still broken. The surgeon put a rod in that bone to hold that leg together until that leg mends itself. Don't let the fact that he's wearing that uniform fool you. He may be smiling, out on the court, and shooting jumpers; but inside, he's still broken."

When you see Christians who are up front in the spotlight preaching, teaching, coaching, or whatever it might be, don't put too much in that. Some of them have been broken by their fathers, in their homes, in their relationships, and in many other ways; but Jesus, the Great Physician, has put the Holy Spirit into their hearts to hold them together so they won't fall apart until they can mend on the inside.

Look Beyond Daddy

Look again at 2 Kings 22:2. Speaking about Josiah, the verse says that he "walked in all the ways of David his father." You remember that we already learned in the previous chapter of 2 Kings that Josiah's father was Amon. But here it's saying that David was his father. What's the explanation for this incongruity?

Amon was Josiah's natural father. But King David was one of Josiah's ancestors, and he would have been proud of Josiah because he was a man after David's own heart. Even though Josiah's father did evil in the sight of God, Josiah did not follow in his steps. Instead, he went back to his ancestry and found someone who could help him—someone who could be his role model, someone whose example he could follow so that he could live his life rightly before God.

Josiah would not have known about David if someone had not told him. Maybe someone said to him, "Stop tripping over your father and look at your ancestor, the great King David. Let me tell you about this giant-killer. Let me tell you about this songwriter. Let me tell you about the one who didn't simply kill thousands of enemies in battle, but tens of thousands. Let me tell you about the greatest king Israel has ever known. He is in your bloodline. You are related to him. Don't focus on the losers in your life. Instead, focus on those who succeeded and follow their example."

Likewise, our fathers may have been messed up, but we should go beyond them and find other men we can respect and pattern our lives after. We may have to search for a while, but all of us men need to find those male role models we can look up to. It may be great men in our families, communities, or ancestries. At any rate, we just need to find at least one man who can teach us what it means to be a man. Some of us don't want to walk like our fathers, so we have to look beyond them and find someone else who can be there for us and help us through our brokenness.

Josiah was raised by his mother, but he walked like his father David. If we don't find that male role model to show us how to be a man, we may become so close to our mothers that we begin to walk like them, talk like them, dress like them, and act like them. Yet even though we've been raised by women, we need to walk like men.

The Bible and the Church

After Josiah became king, he developed his spirituality. In verse 3 of 2 Kings 22, Josiah repaired the temple of God. In verse 8, he found the Book. In contrast, some of us have found the church, but not the Book. We're grateful for the church, but we need the Book as well. Psalm 119:105 says, "Your word is a lamp for my feet, a light on my path." Psalm 1:1-2 tells us, "Blessed is the one who does not walk in step with the wicked or stand in the way that sinners take or sit in the company of mockers, but whose delight is in the law [the Word] of the LORD, and who meditates on his law day and night." We have to get in the Word, read the Word, study the Word, commit to the Word, and let that Word be a lamp to our feet and a light to our pathway.

At the same time, we need the church. David said, "I was glad when they said unto me, 'Let us go into the house of the Lord'" (Psalm 122:1). The writer of Hebrews said, "Don't forsake the assembling of yourselves together as some do" (10:25). Some say, "I don't have to go to church to be a Christian." No, and your car doesn't have to go to someone's gas station to be a car. But if it's going to keep running, it needs to be filled up with gas.

Josiah's church was not perfect. It had problems and had to be rebuilt. There aren't any perfect churches today either, but we don't claim to be perfect. We serve as a hospital for sick souls. Every week we go to the hospital because there is something spiritually wrong with us and we need more of the Holy Spirit working within us so that we can become kings one day. When Jesus returns, He isn't coming for clubs, lodges, or any other organization. He's coming back for the church, which is His people who will reign with Him in glory.

Know How to
Get Home

My second son is a student at Georgetown University, majoring in sports education. I'm proud of Jordan and my other sons as well. They are all doing great. Now, Jordan has always wanted to be a big baller and a shot caller—even when he was little. When he was in the fifth grade, he went with his class on a field trip. He jumped on the bus with the rest of the students from his class, and they were taken downtown to one of the most popular radio station studios in our city. Guy Black was a friend of our family and a popular radio personality there.

Later on, Jordan told his mother and me that as he was riding the bus downtown, he told all of his friends that when it was time to come back, he wasn't riding the bus with the rest of them. Name-dropping in the fifth grade, he said, "I'm going to have Guy Black take me home."

When he was telling us this, his mother said, "Jordan, he doesn't know where we live." We had just moved out to the suburbs, and it was quite a distance from our former home.

Jordan replied, "But I was going to tell him where we live."

Sharon said, "Jordan, *you* don't know where we live."

"Yes, Mommy. I know how to get home."

We were downtown at the time, and Sharon said, "Okay, Jordan. Starting from here, tell me how to get home."

He answered, "Well...Mommy, I don't know how to get home from *here*, but if you take me to the church, I can get home from there."

When we lose our way and we're ready to give up, we can get direction, deliverance, and power at the church. We need the church to find our way home.

Becoming Kings

God has amazing plans for each of our lives. Sadly, too many men reach the end of their lives without ever finding out what that plan was. They go from day to day just letting life happen to them. They never reach out and tap into the power of the Holy Spirit, which is available to all those who have received Jesus as their Lord and Savior. Instead, they are content to wallow in the muddy ponds of "If Only," "I Can't," and "Poor Me." Whenever someone suggests that their lives could be different, they just become angry. Their lives are full of unforgiveness and brokenness. Yet, they have never allowed God to bring healing because they would rather hang on to their resentment. Rather than choosing life, they are choosing death.

God has so much more for us than muddy ponds and negative emotions. Reach out to God. Reach out to a man you respect. Reach out to the Word of God. Reach out to the church. Let's reach out of ourselves to all that's waiting to help us—all that God has already prepared to help us become all that He wants us to be. Let's fulfill our destiny. We are not in this alone. Our heavenly Father has not abandoned us. He has never rejected us. He is here—as He has always been—loving us, caring about us, and ready to help us if we would just ask. Let's not waste one more day living as paupers in this world. Let's become the kings God has called us to be.

Other Books by
Jeffrey A. Johnson, Sr.

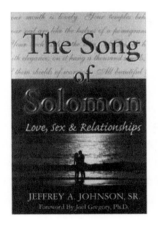

From an ancient love story, we find a message of honesty, hope, and healing for relationships today.

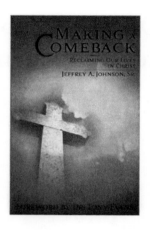

The time for sitting still and bemoaning our lot in life is over. God has empowered us to reclaim what we've lost. We can get our lives back! We can get our health, our minds, our families, and our joy back! We do not have to wallow in defeat. We can make a comeback!

A collection of stories, illustrations, and real-life experiences that help explain the Word of God and make it applicable for everyday life. This book will serve as a daily reminder of God's love, faithfulness, and grace.

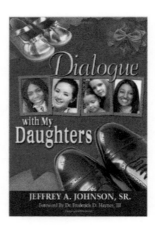

Written from a father's heart, this book covers a variety of topics from learning to appreciate the "you" God created, to knowing what to look for in a mate, to thinking as God thinks. Whatever your age or situation as a woman, this book is for you! (It can also help fathers to know how to have those all-important conversations with their own daughters.)

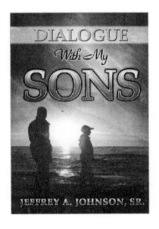

A message from a wise and loving father provides inspiration, practical advice, and frank conversation for young men growing up in America today.

Combining lessons he learned growing up in a single-parent household with lessons from the Word of God, Pastor Johnson shows that God desires to help single parents do more than just survive in their circumstances—He wants them to thrive.